Reaching

for the

Mainland

& SELECTED NEW POEMS

Bilingual Press/Editorial Bilingüe

General Editor
Gary D. Keller

Managing Editor
Karen S. Van Hooft

Associate Editors
Ann Waggoner Aken
Theresa Hannon

Assistant Editor
Linda St. George Thurston

Editorial Board
Juan Goytisolo
Francisco Jiménez
Eduardo Rivera
Mario Vargas Llosa

Address:
Bilingual Press
Hispanic Research Center
Arizona State University
P.O. Box 872702
Tempe, Arizona 85287-2702
(602) 965-3867

REACHING

FOR THE

MAINLAND

& SELECTED NEW POEMS

JUDITH ORTIZ COFER

Bilingual Press/Editorial Bilingüe
TEMPE, ARIZONA

ISBN 0-927534-55-X

Library of Congress Cataloging-in-Publication Data

Ortiz Cofer, Judith, 1952-
      Reaching for the mainland and selected new poems / by Judith Ortiz Cofer.
            p.   cm.
      ISBN 0-927534-55-X (pbk. : alk. paper)
      1. Puerto Rican women—Poetry.   2. Puerto Ricans—Poetry.
      3. Puerto Rico—Poetry.   I. Title.
      PS3565.R7737R43 1995
      811'.54—dc20   95-31050
                                                                  CIP

PRINTED IN THE UNITED STATES OF AMERICA

Cover design by Bidlack Creative Services

Back cover photo by John Cofer

Acknowledgments

The author wishes to express her gratitude to the Florida Fine Arts Council, Division of Cultural Affairs, for a fellowship that allowed her to finish this book.

Acknowledgment is made to the following publications in which some of the poems included in Reaching for the Mainland first appeared:

Affinities: "Walking to Church," and "Grace Stands in Line for Saturday Confession," in Vol. 3, No. 1 (1980); The Florida Arts Gazette: "Baptism at La Misión," in Vol. 3, Issue 9 (1980); Hispanics in the United States: An Anthology of Creative Literature, eds. Gary Keller and Francisco Jiménez (Ypsilanti, MI: Bilingual Press, 1980): "My Father in the Navy," and "En mis ojos no hay días"; Kalliope: "Lesson One: I Would Sing," in Vol. 4, No. 3 (1982); Kansas Quarterly: "To My Brother, Lately Missed," and "The Way My Mother Walked," in Vol. 15, No. 1 (1983); The Louisville Review: "Housepainter," in No. 12 (1982); New Collage: "She Has Been a Long Time Dying," in Vol. 14, No. 2 (1983); New Letters: "Room at the Empire," in Vol. 50, No. 1 (1983).

Acknowledgments continue on page 77.

CONTENTS

Reaching for the Mainland

Selected New Poems

And the tongue is a fire.   –James 3:6

Reaching for the Mainland

The Birthplace

THEY SAY

They say
when I arrived,
traveling light,
the women who waited
plugged
the cracks in the walls
with rags
dipped in alcohol
to keep drafts and demons out.
Candles were lit
to the Virgin.
They say
Mother's breath
kept blowing them out
right and left.
When I slipped
into their hands
the room was in shadows.
They say
I nearly turned away,
undoing
the hasty knot of my umbilicus.
They say
my urge to bleed
told them I was like a balloon
with a leak,
a soul trying to fly away
through the cracks in the wall.
The midwife sewed
and the women prayed
as they fitted
me for life

in a tight corset of gauze.
But their prayers
held me back,
the bandages held me in,
and all that night
they dipped
their bloody rags.
They say
Mother slept through it all,
blowing out
candles
with her breath.

THE WOMAN WHO WAS LEFT AT THE ALTAR

She calls her shadow Juan,
looking back often as she walks.
She has grown fat, her breasts huge
as reservoirs. She once opened her blouse
in church to show the silent town
what a plentiful mother she could be.
Since her old mother died, buried in black,
she lives alone.
Out of the lace she made curtains for her room,
doilies out of the veil. They are now
yellow as malaria.
She hangs live chickens from her waist to sell,
walks to the town swinging her skirts of flesh.
She doesn't speak to anyone. Dogs follow
the scent of blood to be shed. In their hungry,
yellow eyes she sees his face. She takes him
to the knife time after time.

HOUSEPAINTER

The flecks are deeply etched
into the creases of his fingers,
and the paint will not wash off.
It was a hilltop house he painted last
for an old woman going blind
who wanted it to blend into the sky.
It took him two weeks working alone,
and the blue, a hue too dark,
stood out against the horizon
like a storm cloud, but since clouds
had also gathered over her eyes,
she never knew.
He explained his life to me,
a child on my grandfather's lap concerned
with his speckled hands only because they kept me
from my treasure hunting in his painter's shed,
where cans on shelves spilled enamel over
their lids like tears running down a clown's face.

LA TRISTEZA

Books. By reading them,
by writing them, he thinks he has escaped
the sadness of his race.
When he returns to the old town,
open like a violated tomb, bleached bones
exposed to the sun, he walks bareheaded
among the people, to show his disdain
for the sombrero, the hat that humbles.
He has grown somber and pale
in the New England winter, ashamed
of the mahogany skin, the yellow teeth
of the men who move slow as iguanas
in the desert. When they greet him,
their eyes roll up to heaven, each claiming
to have been his father's most intimate friend.
Here they never let go of their dead.
And the women: timid blackbirds, lower
their eyes in his presence.
*Damn the humility of the poor that keeps them
eating dust.* He thinks this, even as he takes
the girl with skin supple as suede to his hotel,
where her body spreading under him is a dark stain
on the clean white sheets he has earned.

MOONLIGHT PERFORMANCE

The pond opens up to the hill
like a woman's vanity mirror.
The naked figure poised on a branch
overhanging the water steps into the moonlight;
he sees lights like a maniac's eyes darting
through the trees playing
frenzied peek-a-boo with him.
As the train rounds the last corner,
he can make out dozens of faces peering
into the night
supplying him with a moving audience,
the engine, with the music and thunder
necessary for a feat of daring.
He bounces and leaps as the headlight
suspends him in space,
completing the performance.

ON THE ISLAND I HAVE SEEN

Men cutting cane under a sun relentless
as an overseer with a quota,
measuring their days
with each swing of their machetes,
mixing their sweat with the sugar
destined to sweeten half a continent's coffee.

Old men playing dominoes in the plazas
cooled by the flutter of palms,
divining from the ivory pieces
that clack like their bones, the future
of the children who pass by on their way to school,
ducklings following the bobbing beak
of the starched nun who leads them in silence.

Women in black dresses keeping all the holy days,
asking the priest in dark confessionals
what to do about the anger in their sons' eyes.
Sometimes their prayers are answered
and the young men take their places
atop the stacked wedding cakes.
The ones who are lost to God and mothers
may take to the fields, the dry fields,
where a man learns the danger or words,
where even a curse can start a fire.

THE MULE

I have been loyal for too long.
My master is gone, and his son
gazes at me with the eyes of a stranger;
he does not touch me in friendship
but prods me in contempt,
and I must carry his burdens joylessly
up and down this mountainside.
My eyes no longer see the rocks
in my path as clearly,
yet each step takes me closer
to the place I have chosen
on a perfect and unyielding road,
no matter who leads.

THE MAN WHO LOST HIS HANDWRITING

There are some who remember Andrés
when he still had words. In my mother's day
he was town scribe, directing every event
with pen and ink.
Legends arose that Don Andrés
was touched by God. Women came to him
before naming their children, searching
his letters like the tarot for symbols. My aunt
was christened Clorinda del Carmen because he gave
the C's the wings of an angel. Andrés also sealed deaths
with his eternal black ink. Don Gonzalo,
the priest, had been heard to say
that even Saint Peter would be pleased to let
a soul into paradise with such a pass.

It was words, they say, that broke Andrés. Two wars
in two decades, reams of telegrams to transcribe from blue
to black; all the letters he had written for the town's sons
stacked on his desk like a tombstone.
Until letter by letter, he lost his alphabet. In time,
he forgot the location of his office.

Andrés now scans the streets like a black periscope
for the bright things he collects:
Foil, glass, nails—anything
that catches the sun.
When he finds what he needs,
he files it away in its proper pocket.

WOMAN WATCHING SUNSET

Sitting on the steps of her clapboard house,
she has only to lift her eyes
to encompass all of her world,
as familiar to her as her own reflection.
The clothes on the line sway
to the wind's whispered waltz,
the dog lies limp in the shade,
one paw throbbing in dream pursuit.
Under the shadow of an old oak
leaning over them like a bored chaperone,
the begonias in their clay pots
are shy girls waiting to be asked to dance.
This is the best time,
when her corner of God's earth is held
in the fingertips of the retreating sun.
And tomorrow she will create her world again,
from scratch.

GRACE STANDS IN LINE FOR SATURDAY CONFESSION

I have knelt to them,
pressing my breasts hard against
their confessional walls.
I have issued them the challenge
of my mortal sins,
imagining them bound
to my secret voice.
I have watched their moist fingers slip
from bead to bead
on their worn-down-to-the-wood rosaries,
and I have listened to the heavy sighs
of their unctuous absolutions.
I have dared to remind them of the darkness
in the cathedral, the pungency of flesh,
that no scented candle can conceal.

WHAT THE GYPSY SAID TO HER CHILDREN

We are like the dead,
invisible to those
who do not want to see,
and our only protection against
the killing silence of their eyes is color:
the crimson of our tents pitched
like a scream
in the fields of our foes,
the amber of our fires
where we gather to lift our voices
in the purple lament of our songs.
And beyond the scope of their senses
where all colors blend into one,
we will build our cities of light,
we will carve them
out of the granite of their hatred,
with our own brown hands.

PUEBLO WAKING

Roosters call their blood back
from claws wrapped around a post, the dog
stretched under the mango tree stirs
dust into the sunlight as he rises, tin roofs
clamor under the first wave of heat like teapots.
Windows thrown wide, voices are tossed back
and forth, picking up talk where it was
interrupted by the night.
At seven, the church bells sound hollow
after their long silence. Old women in black veils climb
the church steps in single file, like a trail
of worker ants.
                    In August, penitents travel
from all parts of the island to this pueblo
to drag bloody knees up the two hundred steps
hewn out of a hillside to the shrine
of the Black Virgin, La Monserrate.
At her feet they leave jewelry and bolts of cloth
for the sisters to make vestments. Many
of the pilgrims have dreams after their visits—numbers
and colors to decipher during the year.
                    But on this day,
Christ's Mother's name is a lament over the late hour,
a plea to hurry to work, to school, to the store
for la leche. Noise rises like an approaching train
until the morning goes round the bend
in a complication of smells
with black beans boiling over the coffee's last call,
as the sting of the midday sun begins to wrap the pueblo
in the silence of siesta.

VISITING LA ABUELA

Called in early to soak the day's play from my skin,
slick as a newborn kitten, to slip into my crinolines,
in my pink parachute dress, to descend on La Abuela,
who once a month waited for her generations to come
                                                    listen.
In her incense-sweet room, we'd sip cocoa,
sitting straight-backed on a sofa that insisted we sink.
I'd watch the old woman's hands,
folded like fledgling sparrows on her lap,
swoop up to tuck a curl under her cap,
and drop again as if too weak to fly for long.
We'd listen to her tales, complex as cobwebs, until,
at a sign from Mother, who paid these visits like giving alms,
I'd kiss the cheek lined like a map to another time,
and grasping Mother's steady hand,
I'd rush us out into the sunlight.

THE GUSANO OF PUERTO RICO

Earthworm, orange as a sunset
over the brown hills of this island,
you surface for food only to become
the tender treat of yellow ants
who climb your back
as you bend your head like a servile camel
to their stings.
Curled around your soft middle,
eyes buried in your body's spiral,
you know your end.
You assume the pose of martyr, but deep
in the warm mud you have left your plentiful,
wriggling seed—more gusanos than mandibles
can crush, opening their eyes in the dark,
without knowledge of sky and sun,
but with the mortal need to seek the light.

THE FRUIT VENDOR

A skeletal man pushing a cart
bright as a carnival, one-eared Gacho
winds his way through town.
Children follow his red and blue hand-wagon,
trying to grab the brass bells on a rope,
mocking his high-pitched call
of, frutas hoy, y viandas.
Once he had been a player of stringed instruments
but lost his left ear and hand to the swing
of a man's machete over a woman's choice of songs.

        The matron in a stained smock
who now moves slow to his call, belly swollen
by childbirth, was courted in her youth
to Gacho's boleros.

At each stop he changes the arrangement:
finding the ripest fruit, he places it on top,
the spiny breadfruit chaperone the tender bananas,
the green plantains are soldiers on leave
surrounding the blushing mangoes. Then he stands back
and waits for the women to arrive like the despoiling army,
ignoring the harmony of his design
with their random selections.

THE SOURCE

Framed in the doorway of her clapboard house,
Vieja sits in her cane rocker waiting
for the coffee trees to rise to her sight
like red-eyed soldiers startled by the sun's reveille,
and this world-wake belongs to her.

Early shadows condense to reveal a flamboyant tree
heavy with blossoms, leaning over the well
that helped her nurse her generations,
and her progeny have been like the sunflower
rather than the rose, scattering their seed.

Yet it all remains fast on this hill,
this house, the well, herself gathering memories
like grandchildren to her lap, to watch the day
climb the hill like her man did so many seasons ago,
bringing the night on his clothes and on his hands.

LETTER FROM A CARIBBEAN ISLAND

This island is a fat whore lolling
tremulous and passive in the lukewarm sea.
Nature has shamed us like a voluptuous daughter:
no place to hide from the debauchery
of sun, wind and vegetation.
All roads end in the sea,
and the mountains are like a garment
shrunk by the heat.
We are hungry for white, longing for snow.
So much color corrupts the soul.
We pray for a different weather, a civil storm,
one that won't enter our homes
like a soldier drunk on blood.
How can we be good Christians here?
In this tropical Eden we sleep on beds
soaked in sweat and spend our days
under a demanding sun that saps
our good intentions.
There are no puritans here.
We throw open our windows to conceive,
letting the western wind blow life into the seed.
Sinners all, we pass the time as best we can
in paradise, waiting for the bridge across the water.

THE BIRTHPLACE

There is no danger now
that these featureless hills
will hold me.
That church
sitting on the highest one
like a great hen
spreading her marble wings
over the penitent houses
does not beckon to me.
This dusty road under my feet
is like any other road
I have traveled,
it leads only
to other roads.
Towns everywhere are the same
when shadows thicken.
Yet, each window
casting a square of light,
that grassy plain under a weighted sky
turning to plum,
tell me
that as surely as my dreams are mine,
I must be home.

The Crossing

MOTHER DANCING IN THE DARK

(And Father somewhere in the Pacific)
She places the needle gently into the worn groove
and a Mexican tenor strains over the violins,
Bésame, bésame mucho . . .
a Mariachi band backs up his demand,
as Mother sinks into the sofa.
From our bed where she has left me
moored to a dreamless sleep, I watch her
rise over her black skirt
like the ballerina in my lacquered music-box,
Como si fuera esta noche la última vez . . .
lift her cheek to a phantom kiss,
Que tengo miedo perderte, bésame, bésame mucho . . .
then bound to the refrain she turns, turns into the shadows
where she is lost to my sight,
(And Father somewhere in the Pacific.)

CROSSINGS

Step on a crack.
In a city of concrete it is impossible
to avoid disaster indefinitely.
You spend your life peering
downward, looking for flaws,
but each day more and more fissures
crisscross your path, and like the lines
on your palms, they mean something
you cannot decipher.
Finally, you must choose between
standing still in the one solid spot you
have found, or you keep moving
and take the risk:
Break your mother's back.

MY FATHER IN THE NAVY

Stiff and immaculate
in the white cloth of his uniform
and a round cap on his head like a halo,
he was an apparition on leave from a shadow-world
and only flesh and blood when he rose from below
the waterline where he kept watch over the engines
and dials making sure the ship parted the waters
on a straight course.
Mother, Brother, and I kept vigil
on the nights and dawns of his arrivals,
watching the corner beyond the neon sign of a quasar
for the flash of white, our father like an angel
heralding a new day.
His homecomings were the verses
we composed over the years making up
the siren's song that kept him coming back
from the bellies of iron whales
and into our nights
like the evening prayer.

ARRIVAL

When we arrived, we were expelled
like fetuses
from the warm belly of an airplane.
Shocked by the cold,
we held hands as we skidded
like new colts on the unfamiliar ice.
We waited winter in a room sealed
by our strangeness.
Watching the shifting tale of the streets,
our urge to fly toward the sun
etched in nailprints like tiny wings
in the gray plaster of the windowsill,
we hoped all the while
that lost in the city's monochrome
there were colors we couldn't yet see.

LATIN WOMEN PRAY

Latin women pray
in incense-sweet churches;
they pray in Spanish to an Anglo God
with a Jewish heritage.

And this Great White Father,
imperturbable in His marble pedestal
looks down upon His brown daughters,
votive candles shining like lust
in His all-seeing eyes,
unmoved by their persistent prayers.

Yet year after year,
before his image they kneel,
Margarita, Josefina, María and Isabel,
all fervently hoping
that if not omnipotent,
at least He be bilingual.

THE WAY MY MOTHER WALKED

She always wore an amulet on a gold chain,
an ebony fist
to protect her from the evil eye of envy
and the lust of men.
She was the gypsy queen of Market Street,
shuttling her caramel-candy body past
the blind window of the Jewish tailor
who did not lift his gaze,
the morse code of her stiletto heels sending
their Mayday-but-do-not-approach into
the darkened doorways where eyes
hung like mobiles in the breeze.
Alleys
made her grasp my hand teaching me
the braille of her anxiety.
The two flights to our apartment were her holy ascension
to a sanctuary from strangers where evil
could not follow on its caterpillar feet and where
her needs and her fears could be put away
like matching towels on a shelf.

SCHOOLYARD MAGIC

Leaning on the chain-link fence of P.S. No. 11,
my flesh cracking in the bitter breeze of a December day,
I burrow deep into my clothes and watch the black girls
jump rope so fast and hot my own skin responds.
Red, green, tartan coats balloon up around
longstem legs, making them exotic flowers and birds.
They sing a song to the beat of the slap-slap
of a clothesline on concrete:

> A sailor went to sea, sea, sea,
> To see what he could see, see, see,
> And all that he could see, see, see,
> Was the bottom of the deep, blue,
> Sea, sea, sea. . .

The brick building framing their play,
the rusted fire-escape hanging over their heads,
the black smoke winding above in spirals—
all of it is wished away,
as I let my blood answer the summons of their song,
drawing my hands free from all my winter folds,
I clap until my palms turn red,
joining my voice to theirs,
rising higher than I ever dared.

CLAIMS

Last time I saw her, Grandmother
had grown seamed as a Bedouin tent.
She had claimed the right
to sleep alone, to own
her nights, to never bear
the weight of sex again, or to accept
its gift of comfort, for the luxury
of stretching her bones.
She'd carried eight children,
three had sunk in her belly, náufragos,
she called them, shipwrecked babies
drowned in her black waters.
Children are made in the night and
steal your days
for the rest of your life, amen. She said this
to each of her daughters in turn. Once she had made a pact
with man and nature and kept it. Now like the sea,
she is claiming back her territory.

A PHOTOGRAPH OF MOTHER AT FIFTEEN HOLDING ME

Still honey-melon round
from recent motherhood,
she holds me, a limp thing,
away from her,
like children hold their baby dolls,
smiling down shyly
at her amazing deed.
The dark arms look strong,
not too long away
from playground volleyball.
Her white wedgies face each other
in pigeon-toed uncertainty.

WALKING TO CHURCH

Latin girls don't just walk,
they sway sensuously
to the rhythm
of some secret melody.

Demure as sidewalk Mona Lisas,
eyes cast downward
in mocking modesty
from passersby, attempting to conceal
any intimation of the sudden surges
of their adolescent hearts
that put such spring into their steps.

Moving just behind them
all in black is Mamá,
silent, somber sentinel,
also swaying,
a secret song also
playing
on her mind.

"EN MIS OJOS NO HAY DÍAS"

from Borges's poem
"The Keeper of the Books"

Back before the fire burned behind his eyes
in the blast furnace which finally consumed him,
Father told us about the reign of little terrors
of his childhood, beginning
at birth with his father who cursed him
for being the twelfth and the fairest,
too blond and pretty to be from his loins,
so he named him the priest's pauper son.
Father said the old man kept
a mule for labor
wine in his cellar
a horse for sport
a mistress in town
and a wife to bear him daughters
to send to church
to pray for his soul
and sons,
to send to the fields
to cut the cane
and raise the money
to buy his rum.
He was only ten when he saw his father
split a man in two with his machete
and walk away proud to have rescued his honor
like a true hombre.
Father always wrapped these tales
in the tissue paper of his humor,
and we'd listen at his knees,

rapt, warm and safe
in the blanket of his caring.
But he himself could not be saved.
To this day his friends still ask,
"What on earth drove him mad?"
Remembering Prince Hamlet I reply,
"Nothing on earth,"
but no one listens to ghost stories anymore.

MEMORY OF LA ABUELA

My grandfather tells me
about the first time he saw her,
a brown figure against the sun,
skirt held up as if beginning
a dance, carrying her shoes
in one hand as she crossed her father's pasture,
pausing now and then
to pick a wildflower.
Ending the anecdote, the old man
lowers his eyes and falls deep into silence,
perhaps seeing a young woman gather her skirts
in a green pasture. In the next telling,
she dances.

MEDITATION ON MY HANDS

They are always folding on each other,
scared pink mice or marsupial embryos
seeking a teat.
Your fingers, Mother, were a vise
strong and quick with the sure grip
of the blind,
always finding the tender spot
on my arm to pinch when I had said too much
in front of the company.
But to be fair,
I would never have been a dropped baby,
though your embrace left me marked
with long tapering stripes.
Mother, with those talented hands,
you should have been a pianist, or one
of those Borgia women who strangled
their unfaithful lovers with fingers
like silk threads.

SHE HAS BEEN A LONG TIME DYING

Skin like a crushed paper bag
and a voice like a shovel striking dry ground,
she calls us to come closer as she rises on her elbows
like some skinny bird poised for flight.
We file past her in generations,
looking her over like a museum piece we fear to touch;
smelling the decay, we try to rush
but she will not let go,
pressing her sharp fingers into our flesh,
drawing our mouths to hers,
breathing death into us and calling us
her babies.

TREASURE

It is a sun-blanched day.
His face rises pale as a September moon
over the black suit.
He sits straight-backed on a cement block.
In the background white curtains billow like wings
over his shoulders, or like a summons
to a cool interior. But he is solid against
their movement, staring through
squinting lids past the camera to the field
he would soon harvest, or into the future
at a grandchild he did not live to know, who
has lately found his familiar face glued to the lid
of an old jewelry box, enduring like Spanish gold
among the gaudy trinkets.

The Habit of Movement

THE OTHER

A sloe-eyed dark woman shadows me.
In the morning she sings
Spanish love songs in a high falsetto,
filling my shower stall
with echoes.
She is by my side
in front of the mirror as I slip
into my tailored skirt and she
into her red cotton dress.
She shakes out her black mane as I
run a comb through my closely cropped cap.
Her mouth is like a red bull's eye
daring me.
Everywhere I go I must
make room for her; she crowds me
in elevators where others wonder
at all the space I need.
At night her weight tips my bed, and
it is her wild dreams that run rampant
through my head exhausting me. Her heartbeats,
like dozens of spiders carrying the poison
of her restlessness,
drag their countless legs
over my bare flesh.

ROOM AT THE EMPIRE

It is the hour of the exodus.
From my hotel window I watch the biography
of this day unfold: Two women cross 63rd, burdens
on their arms—on their shoulders they carry
the skins of animals.
In step they enter the delicatessen
where they will meet others of their kind.
Slouched in a doorway a drunk lies unconscious, his boots
jutting up like stone markers in the path of pedestrians.
A couple kiss as they wait for "Walk," a crowd gathers
behind the two, who part faces and join hands.
As in an old newsreel they all move forward at once,
dispersing when they reach the other side.
The drunkard stretches, yawning: The rush is over.
Soon the sun pales, a movie screen before the credits,
and in the gathering mist above Lincoln Center
points of light begin to flicker.
Yellow taxis cruise the boulevard like frantic bees
pollinating the city.
The evening drifts away in waves of traffic.
In the new silence I find
I have tuned my breathing to bells of a distant cathedral.

TO MY BROTHER, LATELY MISSED

Crustaceans from the same waters, we
keep our vessels separate though
the currents have flowed in our way more
often these seasons,

And, as time softens the walls between
our chambers,
the echoes of your life sounds have touched me,
but I, concentrating on my pearl, have chosen
the seclusion of my species,

The moon determines your directions now, brother,
while I remain imbedded
in coral, hoarding my treasure in
the silence of a multitude, alone
in this tenement of captives.

Lost Angels

You may find them in the gray mist
that rises from city sidewalks,
near piles of trash,
like discarded Christmas ornaments.
I have seen them on the frozen clotheslines
of tenements, masquerading
as the long-sleeved shirts of working men
arm-in-arm in a dozen dingy crucifixions,
in the globes of breath
of the park-bench wino sleeping,
in the pink spittle that clings
to his chin like death.
Look for them in the stained plaster
above the insomniac's bed.
It's possible to see them swimming
like a mote in the eyes of a friend
you haven't seen for some time,
who tells you she has heard the wind
calling her name,
who speaks recklessly of the proximity of clouds.

CLOSED CASKET

The bed you slept on was never large enough
for your restless sleep, Father.
After a twelve-to-six shift it was fun
to watch you count down into exhaustion
in starts and jerks as if some mad marionettist
were pulling your limbs with invisible strings.
How does it feel to be sleeping
on this narrow bed?
They have closed the door on you
who never needed privacy to sleep;
you, who took your sleep in boxer's rounds,
waking with glazed and swollen eyes
to an alarm I never heard
no matter how hard I listened.

WE ARE ALL CARRIERS

Now don't think my opinions on this matter are final,
but I believe that we are all
born equipped with a gland of madness,
though its exact location is still unknown;
it hangs in the vault of our skulls
like a pendulum marking time,
thin-skinned like a grape
and popping full of black bile.
In some people it grows into their flesh
like an embryo or a tumor,
in others it swings by a thread exposed
so that a sudden jar or playful shove,
a shrill note or blinding light, will rupture
the delicate membrane causing poison to pour out
like India ink seeping into the brain and
burning away at memory and choice.
From such accidents are snipers made,
and heroes of war.
Most often, though, the damage is minor:
a pinprick leak, slow and almost imperceptible
like the waterdrop that bores a hole into the rock,
accounts for those of us who tread lightly
as we cross the bamboo bridges our enemy
has built in our path,
those of us who daily waver
between writing a poem and slashing our wrists.

IN YUCATÁN

1.

Here all day it is high noon, sun baking people
the color of clay. At Uxmal and Chichén-Itzá I have seen
the profiles of an ancient race carved on the golden
                                                    sandstone
of pyramids; at the hotel in Mérida I see them again, the faces
of desk clerk, bellhop and maid. The woman who makes my
                                                            bed
bends like a priest over the sacrificial altar; the clay figure
of Chac-Mool, the god of rain, sits on the dresser, gazing
at the nape of her neck where she has wound a braid
into a symbol of eternity. Ending her labors she turns,
and I see the Mayan features carved in angles on the solar
                                                        plains,
the calendar stone, of a face certain in the knowledge of its
                                                        past.
"Es todo, Señora," she says. It is all.

2.

Kukulcán crawls. Quetzalcóatl calls. The serpent gods rule
                                                        time.
The Toh bird keeps time with its tufted tail swinging
like a metronome. The Maya knew time, giving each day
a name for centuries past their own fall, which they saw
as clearly as the stars each night reflected on a golden water
                                                        bowl.
The church bells of Mérida call; the Maya also know the
                                                        tongue
of bells. From the window I watch a beggar drag his reluctant
                                                        legs

46

across the cobblestones to the church steps. The women

                                                sweep

by him, a flock of doves in their rebozos. "Caridad,
por Dios, caridad," he calls waving his cane, scattering them.

3.

At dusk the men come in from the fields
where from light to dark they have arced the rows
of the henequen plant in the same pendulum motion
their ancestors used. Civilization is a habit.
At day's end they will enter their clay huts, dank
as caverns when Chac sends the rains, to eat the good
maize, watch the world through the flickering magic
of the televisions, and finally to sleep in hammocks
made from the hemp they have harvested.
Time is a serpent that circles the world.
Once upon a time men the color of clay saw the coming
of men pale as death, pale as the moon that hangs distant
and mute over all of us, this night in Yucatán.

RETURNING FROM THE MAYAN RUINS

On a night thick with the smells of a recent rain,
I drive through an Indian village where lights
from the round clay huts called chozas make it seem
like a jack-o-lantern town where for the stranger driving
through, every night is Halloween.
I inhale the air weighted with smells of the damp earth,
the ripe carcass of a dog I swerve to miss, smouldering
heaps of rubbish at every unexpected bend.
Passing an open doorway I glimpse a family sleeping
in layers, each body cocooned in the webbing of a hammock;
nearest the road is the woman whose braid falls to the dirt
floor like a black rope, on her breast an infant suckles.
Shifting to a more silent gear,
I leave these new Mayas swaying ceaselessly
to the movement of the earth, suspended in a deeper sleep
than their ancestors could have known.

POSTCARD FROM A FOREIGN COUNTRY

So much left out of the picture.
See the little houses gathered
around the cathedral like girls
making their First Communion,
notice how the old church leans
toward the town as if listening
to its whispered confessions.
They say the mortar is crumbling
under the stones.
I am standing in the church's shadow
as I write you this note,
a shadow it has thrown
on this town for centuries,
watching the night erase this scene
like a drawing on a blackboard,
a message scribbled hastily:
only postcard days are forever.

When You Come to My Funeral

for Betty Owen

Bring conga drums and maracas,
meet at the statue in the plaza,
the one of Columbus pointing his index finger at the sky
as if to say, "you have found your way, amigos."
Be there at 3 o'clock, the hour of the siesta,
when the aroma of perking coffee draws laborers
from the fields to the cool shade
of kitchens and cantinas.

Bring your music and board the bus that goes
to the shore where I always wanted to live.
The trail is treacherous and narrow and the driver
will curse the day and embrace the wheel with
his strong brown arms, he was my friend,
invite him down for the party.

There will be rum punch and pasteles,
and if you bring a sad word for me leave it on the porch
like a wet umbrella, or better still, toss it out to sea.
I will be among you gathered at the edge of the Atlantic
to compose a new kind of dirge, one of vigorous beat
and a rocking cadence,
one that will take me out like a favorable current,
into the silence of my new way.

STREET PEOPLE

Miami, 1983

In the mornings you see them
sucked like leeches to the walls
of public buildings, hanging on
against the gale storm
of a night on the streets.
They speak to us
with their bodies' occupation
of pestilence, death
by osmosis, the contagion
of dispossession.
If we must pass them, we brace
ourselves with indifference.
It clings to us like the odor
of garlic. We walk fast,
each of us holding tight
to whatever we most fear to lose.

BECAUSE MY MOTHER BURNED HER LEGS IN A FREAK ACCIDENT

I am flying south over the Atlantic
toward one of those islands
arranged like shoes on a blue carpet.
She lies in bed waiting for the balm
of my presence, her poor legs pink
as plucked hens. When her gas stove exploded
as she bent over her soup, the flames grabbed
her ankles like a child throwing a tantrum.
So she has summoned me transatlantically,
her voice sounding singed as if the fire
had burned her from within.
She wants me there to resurrect her flesh,
to reverse time, to remind her of the elastic
skin that once sustained me.
She wants me to come home and save her,
as only a child who has been forgotten and forgiven can.

PROGRESS REPORT TO A DEAD FATHER

"Keep it simple, keep it short,"
you'd say to me, "Get to the point,"
when the hoard of words I had stored for you
like bits of bright tinsel in a squirrel's nest
distracted you from the simple "I love you"
that stayed at tongue-tip.

Father, I am no more succinct now than when
you were alive; the years have added reams
to my forever manuscript.
Lists rile me now in your stead,
labeled "things to do today" and
"do not forget" lists of things
I will never do, lists that I write
to remind me that I can never forget.

I can still hear you say,
"A place for everything and
everything in its place."
But chaos is my roommate now, Father,
and he entertains often.

Simplicity is for the strong-hearted,
you proved that with your brief
but thorough life. Your days were stacked
like clean shirts in a drawer.
Death was the point you drove home
the day your car met the wall,
your forehead split in two, not in your familiar frown,
but forever—a clean break.
"It was quick," the doctor said. "He didn't feel a thing."

It was not your fault that love could not be
so easily put in its right place
where I could find it when I needed it,
as the rest of your things, Father.

BAPTISM AT LA MISIÓN

"José Juan Pablo González, I anoint you
in the name of all that's holy,
a Christian and one of us."
I hold him high above the ecstatic crowd
in consecration, and he screams in terror
of space. Longing for solitude
and darkness, he hates the drowning and
the hands, the grinning faces,
the voices singing praises.
He wants only to suck his toes,
and wrap his mother's flesh around him.

FEVER

My daughter is burning and may
burst into flames
before night's end.
Pressing her limp fingers to my palm
I will them to curl,
but reflex has been left
on the other side of the hot door.
Fear touches the nape of my neck,
making me reach back through time,
absorbing child into flesh,
to cool her in my waters.

A POEM

for Jim Hall

I wish I could write a poem like the 2:30 sun
that shocks you every afternoon
as if it were a hot shower pouring
over your shoulders through your office window
so that you are forced to leave
the poems you have been tending
while you maneuver the blinds,
turn on the lights, resettle.
I wish I could write an inopportune poem,
one that would make you rise complaining
of the heat and the blinding light.
A poem I would write like a fetish;
an undesirable unavoidable poem,
one that would change your life a little
like the Great Vowel Shift did English,
one that would make you want to get up
in the middle of the night to search
for things you didn't know were lost.

A-1-A

Gulls build their nests on telephone poles,
laying their eggs on the warm terminals.
Could the currents of conversation
become a part of the awakening, subtly changing
the embryos through sounds seeping
into their sacs?
Words of warning of their season: inclement
weather, ships lost at sea, hearts broken
with a click.
The fledgling that fears to trust its instincts
and the wind, wobbling as it perches
over the highway, perhaps listened
too long to the tone of hasty departures, the rise
and fall of voices a warning of the dangers
of flight, the sudden silence a clue
to the message of shells: that nothing lasts.

THE HABIT OF MOVEMENT

Nurtured in the lethargy of the tropics,
the nomadic life did not suit us at first.
We felt like red balloons set adrift
over the wide sky of this new land.
Little by little we lost our will to connect
and stopped collecting anything heavier
to carry than a wish.
We took what we could from books borrowed
in Greek temples, or holes in the city walls,
returning them hardly handled.

We carried the idea of home on our backs
from house to house, never staying
long enough to learn the secret ways of wood
and stone, and always the blank stare
of undraped windows behind us
like the eyes of the unmourned dead.
In time we grew rich in dispossession
and fat with experience.
As we approached but did not touch others,
our habit of movement kept us safe
like a train in motion—
nothing could touch us.

Lesson One: I Would Sing

In Spanish, "cantaría" means I would sing,
"Cantaría bajo de la luna,"
I would sing under the moon.
"Cantaría cerca de tu tumba,"
By your grave I would sing,
"Cantaría de una vida perdida,"
Of a wasted life I would sing,
If I may, if I could, I would sing.
In Spanish the conditional
is the tense of dreamers,
of philosophers, fools, drunkards,
of widows, new mothers, small children,
of old people, cripples, saints, and poets.
It is the grammar of expectation and
the formula for hope; "Cantaría, amaría, viviría,"
Please repeat after me.

Selected New Poems

The Dream of Birth

Her voice as familiar as my own,
scrapes the ocean floor,
coming through ragged with static during the call
from Puerto Rico. She is staying at her sister's house
until she finds a new place for herself—has called
to say she is moving again and to share the horror
prompting her flight.

On the first night of deep sleep in the old house
she had rented back on native soil—a place
she would decorate with our past, where
yellowed photographs of a young man in khaki
army issue (the way she chooses to remember her husband)
and my brother and me as sepia-toned babies in their chipped
                                                    frames,
a place where she could finally begin to collect
her memories like jars of preserves on a shelf—
there, she had lain down to rest on her poster bed centered
in a high-ceilinged room, exhausted from the labor
of her passage, and dreamed
she had given birth to one of us again. She felt the weight
of a moist, wriggling mass on her chest, the greedy mouth
seeking a milk-heavy breast, then suddenly—real pain—

piercing as a newborn infant's cry—yanking her
out of her dream. In the dark she felt the awful heft
of the thing stirring over her. Flipping on the light

she saw, to her horror, a bat clinging to her gown,
its hallucinated eyes staring up from the shroud of black
                                                    wings,

hanging on, hanging on, with perfect little fingers,

                                                                       as she,
wild with fear and revulsion, struggled free of her clothes,
throwing the bundle hard against the wall. By daylight
she had returned to find the rust-colored stain streaked
on the white plaster, and the thing still fluttering
in the belly of the dress. She had dug a tiny grave
with her gardening spade on the spot
where she would have planted roses.

THROUGH CLIMATE CHANGES

He waits
in her widow's living room
where she has not removed
Father's photograph
from its vantage point
on the mantel.

I have traveled all day
through climate changes,
from north to south,
to see her.

On the drive from the airport
she tells me about the man,
who will *never, never*
take my father's place.

I inhale deeply,
the air heavy
with subtropical moisture,
her perfume—his favorite—
now intensified
by the closeness, the heat.
The familiar smells
call up the times
when curled in the backseat
I trusted my parents
to take me
where they would.

Now exhausted and dizzy
from the journey,

I watch my mother's hands
gripping the wheel—
the subtle map of veins
becoming bas-relief, tracing
the same country as mine
clasped on my lap.

As we travel down a road
lined with mango trees,
branches sagging
with the weight of the fruit,
I listen in silence
to her Spanish lament
with its refrain
of sola, triste,
la vida, el amor.
I am defeated
by the beauty of the words,
or simply beaten down
by the blazing sun
magnified through glass.

When we walk into her house,
she turns into a shy girl,
introducing me formally
as if I were a diplomat
from a foreign land,
to the timid man
in a starched, white shirt
embroidered in patterns
I recognize from the past.

The open palm he extends
is both a greeting

and a plea.
Before I respond,
I look up at my father,
stern in his frame,
and I reject the power
granted me by grief.

Instead
I reach for the hand
of this man who loves my mother.

PHOTOGRAPHS OF MY FATHER

On my walls there are three
photographs of my father.
In one he is a young recruit
standing *at ease,*
third from the left
with his platoon.
In another he has rank
on his cap—a formal
pose in a studio,
intended for his mother.
In the last, a blowup
from my mother's wallet
taken by a machine
in a foreign port, he is
a melancholy petty officer
in navy blues. Hazy
like a ghost sighting,
creased from her handling,
it is my favorite.

These are the survivors
from a day of fury. One morning
in my childhood, on his way
out to sea, he had sat
alone in the living room,
and without hurry, with care,
cut himself out of our family.
Book after book.
I watched him work
from my room, knowing
his actions were prelude
or aftermath to family strife.

My mother in the kitchen
holding her coffee cup
with both hands, also waited.

On the floor
my father's image lay
like peelings from an apple.
In his hands the scissors glinted
at the eye and snapped
like a live thing.

Nothing more. Just picture albums
shameful as a vandalized church,
never seen by me again. And years
after his death, my need to find
his face revealed in innocence,
unguarded, as I never knew it.
This vulnerable young man, this face
that fills me with grief and longing.
I am trying to believe in this boy.

LETTER FROM HOME IN SPANISH

She writes to me as if we still shared
the same language. The page
a laden sky, filled with flying letters
suspended just above the lines
like blackbirds on the horizon;
the accents—something smaller
they are pursuing.

                    She says:
"after a lifetime of tending to people,
our vieja is obsessed
with useless endeavors—raising fat hens
she refuses to eat, letting them live
until their feathers droop and drag
on the dirt, like the hems
of slovenly women.

        "Listen,"
she writes, forgetting that the words
cannot pull me by the elbow, "she will not pick
the roses she grows, so that walking
through her garden is like following a prostitute—
the smell chokes you; makes you
want to loosen your dress.

        "She fills her house with old things:
baby pictures she misnames, mistaking me
for you; undoing the generations; yellowed ads
for beauty products and clothes; headlines
from the War; her last child's obituary—
the one who never tasted sugar,
then died of something simple.

"She has no use now
for those of us who survived. The other women
and I take turns at her side, but if we burn
a light in the dark rooms she prefers,
she covers her face as if ashamed.
If we dust the picture frames, she claims
we are trying to erase the past.

"But, basta. Enough for now."

I read her letter aloud, for the sound
of Spanish, and it becomes a kyrie,
a litany in a mass for the dead.
I take each vowel on my tongue.
La vieja brings tears to my eyes
like incense; *la muerte*
sticks in my throat like ashes.

Her blessing is a row of black crosses
on a white field.

Three Poems in Memory of Mamá
(Grandmother)

COLD AS HEAVEN

Before there is a breeze again
before the cooling days of Lent, she may be gone.
My grandmother asks me to tell her
again about the snow.
We sit on her white bed
in this white room, while outside
the Caribbean sun winds up the world
like an old alarm clock. I tell her
about the enveloping blizzard I lived through
that made everything and everyone the same;
how we lost ourselves in drifts so tall
we fell through our own footprints;
how wrapped like mummies in layers of wool
that almost immobilized us, we could only
take hesitant steps like toddlers
toward food, warmth, shelter.
I talk winter real for her,
as she would once conjure for me to dream
at sweltering siesta time,
cool stone castles in lands far north.
Her eyes wander to the window,
to the teeming scene of children
pouring out of a yellow bus, then to the bottle
dripping minutes through a tube
into her veins. When her eyes return to me,
I can see she's waiting to hear more
about the purifying nature of ice,
how snow makes way for a body,

how you can make yourself an angel
by just lying down and waving your arms
as you do when you say
good-bye.

THE BODY KNOWS

The doctor's hands
leave my grandmother frozen
to the sheets, shivering.
The well-chosen words of her children
make her button her robe to her neck.
She asks for more cover, for a sweater
and socks, though the Puerto Rican sun
slashes through venetian blinds
defeating the a.c., wilting the petals
so the roses hang over the rim
as if they had fainted in their vase.

The old woman cannot be made warm.
The vital signs screens inform her
of the coming of winter, a foreign season
the body knows,
and she is preparing to step out
into the breath-stopping cold.

NOCHE NUEVE

I rush in from a standby day of flights
in time for the last of a twelve-rosary novena,
a purgatory for the survivors gathered in this last gasp
of a scorching summer to help Mamá's soul escape
the field of thorny bushes somewhere between earth
and heaven, where her white cotton slip
may have gotten snagged on her way up.

The tireless rezadora, hired at a weekly wage
to lead us in the loops of Hail Marys, counts off
sets on her worn wooden beads, speaks
Mamá's given name, without the Doña
she earned in this life,
for she is now a naked spirit like the rest.
One of us always starts up or sighs, rudely awakened
from the lull of repetition by the too-familiar words
spoken by a stranger. But no one may object:
we are negotiating for the key to the comfortable room
where our tired matriarch will spend eternity. If only
we can say it enough times,
God, the gatekeeper, Mary, the housemother, Saint Peter,
the hard-of-hearing custodian of the garden
of rare white orchids, the kind she spent a lifetime
yearning to cultivate, may respond. Then
maybe we can rise
from our hard folding chairs branded with the name
of the funeral home, to be returned. We can toast
her memory with the customary hot chocolate and crackers,
kiss her photo on the little altar of wilting tropical flowers
from her backyard and the FDS bouquets

called in by mainland descendants,
all the blossoms now equally redolent
as flores para los muertos; and go home
to face our private grief.

Acknowledgments Continued

New Mexico Humanities Review: "Latin Women Pray," in Vol. 4, No. 1 (1981); *Nosotras: Latina Literature Today,* eds. María del Carmen Boza, Beverly Silva, and Carmen Valle (Binghamton, N.Y.: Bilingual Press, 1986): "The Other," and "They Say"; *Orphic Lute:* "Treasure," in Spring Issue (1984); *The Panhandler:* "We Are All Carriers," in No. 13 (1983); *The Pawn Review:* "Because My Mother Burned Her Legs in a Freak Accident," in Vol. 15 (1984); *Poets On:* Barriers: "Meditation on My Hands," Vol. 8, No.1 (1984); *Prairie Schooner:* "The Woman Who Was Left at the Altar," and "Claims," in Vol. 59, No. 1 (1985); *St Croix Review:* "Woman Watching Sunset," and "A Photograph of Mother at Fifteen Holding Me," in Vol. 15, No. 2 (1982); *South Florida Poetry Review:* "Closed Casket," in Vol. 1, No. 2 (1984); *Southern Humanities Review:* "Moonlight Performance," in Vol. 6, No. 3 (1982); *Southern Poetry Review:* "In Yucatán," and "Returning from the Mayan Ruins," in Vol. 23, No. 2 (1983) and "La Tristeza," in Vol. 24, No. 2 (1984); *Tendril:* "Letter from a Caribbean Island," in Seventh Anniversary Issue, No. 19-20 (1985); *Woman of Her Word: Hispanic Women Write,* ed. Evangelina Vigil (Houston: Arte Publico Press, 1983): "What the Gypsy Said To Her Children," and "Progress Report To A Dead Father." In addition, several poems in this book were first part of a limited edition chapbook, *The Native Dancer* (Bourbonnais, IL: Pteranodon Press,1981).

Acknowledgment is made to the following publications in which some of the poems included in *Selected New Poems* first appeared:

Southern Poetry Review: "The Dream of Birth," in Vol. 29, 1989; *Prairie Schooner:* "Letter From Home in Spanish," and "Photographs of My Father," in Vol. 66, No.31 (1992) and in the Winter 1994 issue, respectively. Reprinted from *Prairie Schooner* by permission of the University of Nebraska Press. Copyrighted 1992 and 1994 University of Nebraska Press.